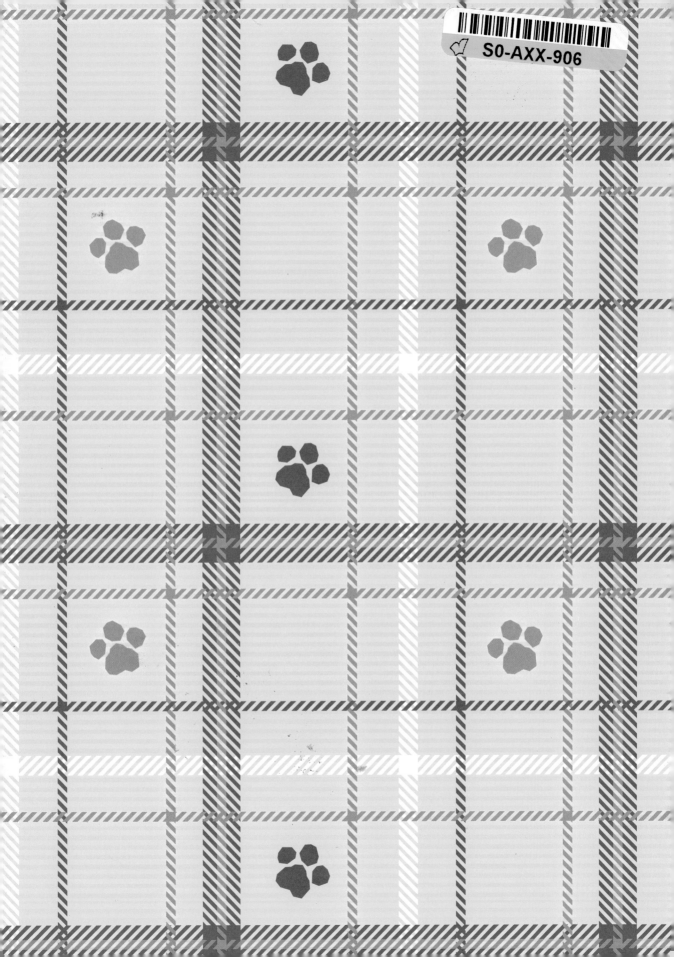

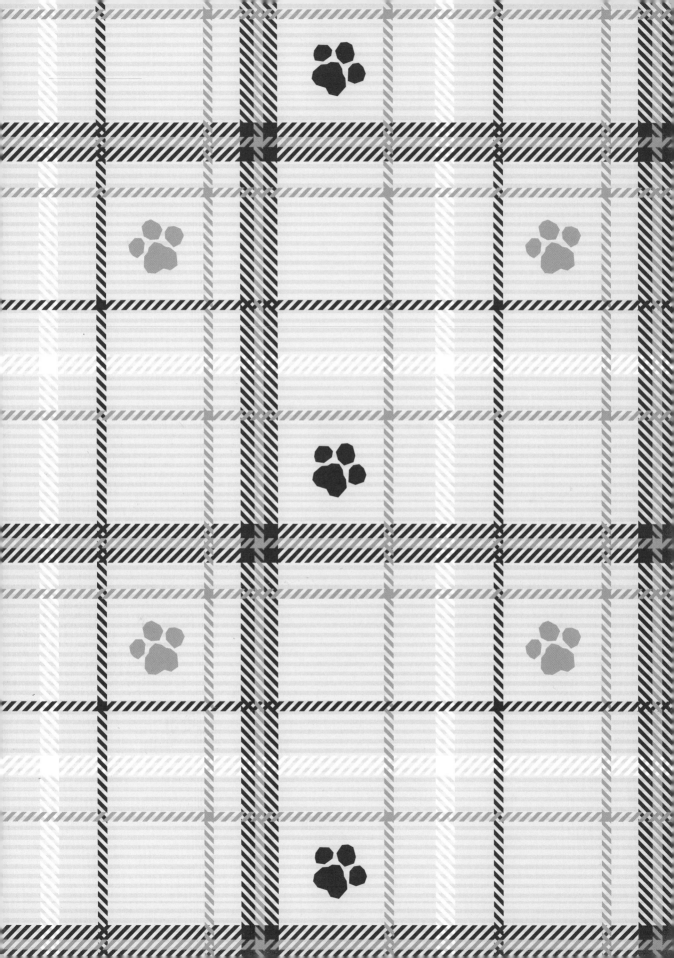

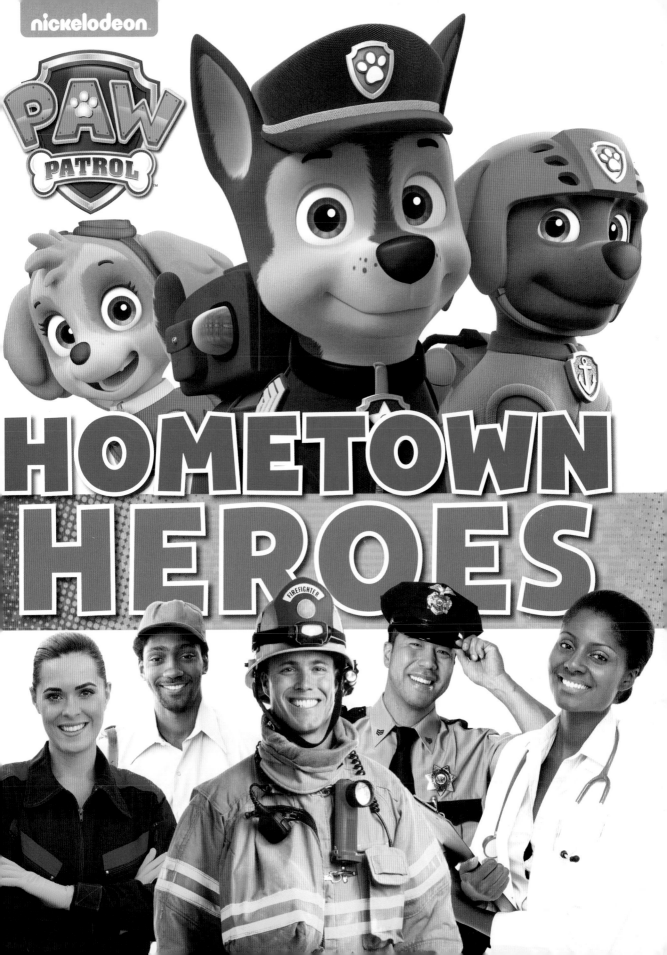

nickelodeon

PAW PATROL

HOMETOWN HEROES

In Adventure Bay, the PAW Patrol is always ready for a ruff ruff rescue. But did you know your hometown has a lot of heroes, too? Meet all the different people in your community who are always ready to save the day!

Contents

Police Officers

They keep the peace!

Police officers have a lot of important jobs in the community. They make sure everyone follows the law and they help in emergencies. Police officers do their best to keep everyone safe.

These paws uphold the laws!

Radio!

Hat!

Badge

PUPPY PUNCHLINE

Why did the police officer go to the baseball game?

He heard that someone had stolen a base!

5

Paramedics

They give emergency medical treatment!

Paramedics and EMTs are medical professionals. They drive ambulances and help people who are sick. They get people to the hospital fast!

Paramedics can drive super fast!

Medical Bag!

Gloves!

Reflective Jacket!

Did You Know? EMT stands for emergency medical technician!

7

Doctors

They help sick and hurt people!

Doctors help people stay healthy! They give medicine to sick people, fix broken bones, give people advice on how to take care of themselves, and a whole lot more!

Doctors do their best to make everyone feel better!

PUPPY PUNCHLINES!

Why did the banana go to the doctor?

Because it wasn't peeling well!

Stethoscope!

Lab Coat!

Clipboard!

9

Veterinarians

They keep animals healthy!

Animals need to get checkups, too! Animal doctors are called veterinarians or vets for short. They help sick animals everywhere!

A vet will take good care of your pet!

Stethoscope!

Scrubs!

Did You Know?
Some vets specialize in awesome animals like elephants, monkeys, and even tigers!

Patient!

11

Crossing Guards

They help you get to the other side!

Crossing guards make sure everyone gets across the street safely and have signs to tell cars to stop and let people pass!

GREEN means go and RED means stop!

Stop Sign!

STOP

Reflective Vest!

Whistle!

PUPPY PUNCHLINE

What do you say to a frog that needs a ride?

¡Hop in!

Teachers

They help us learn!

Teachers help make our community a better place by educating every kid who comes to class. They teach people how to read and write, do math, perform science experiments and a lot more!

This pup is ready to learn!

Dry-Erase Board!

Markers!

Text Book!

PUPPY PUNCHLINE

Why did the teacher wear sunglasses?

Because the students were so bright!

15

Librarians

They help you find information!

Librarians help people find books, magazines and information online. They have a system to keep books organized so you can always find what you need!

I'm ruff-ruff ready to research!

PUPPY PUNCHLINES!

What kind of book does a rabbit like to read?

One with a hoppy ending!

Scanner!

Books!

Computer!

17

Lifeguards

They keep you safe in the water!

Lifeguards work at pools and on beaches. Their job is to make sure that everyone is safe while they're swimming.

Lifeguards are always ready to dive in!

Binoculars!

Swimsuit!

Did You Know?

Lifeguards are trained to rescue people and know CPR!

Rescue Can!

19

Park Rangers

They protect our national parks!

Park rangers help protect national parks. They spot and put out forest fires, help injured animals get medical treatment, give tours of the parks and teach people about wildlife.

There are 417 national parks in the United States!

Did You Know?

Kids can join the National Park Service as junior rangers!

USNPS

Hat!

Badge!

Park Information!

Yellowstone

Construction Workers

They build and fix things!

Construction workers build really long bridges, super tall buildings, airports, roads, tunnels—just about everything! They work with a lot of sharp and heavy tools, so they wear special clothes to protect themselves.

Let's dig it!

Hard Hat!

Reflective Vest!

Tool Belt!

PUPPY PUNCHLINES!

How does a penguin build its house?

Igloos it together!

23

Mail Carriers

They bring you your mail!

Neither rain, snow, sleet nor hail can keep your mail carrier away! These dependable delivery people make sure you get your packages and letters.

Letter carriers work in the snow, just like me!

24

Did You Know?

Before they had trucks, some mail carriers used to deliver mail by riding on horses!

Mail Bag!

Uniform!

Letters!

25

Sanitation Workers

They keep your hometown clean!

Sanitation workers, also known as trash collectors, ride in garbage trucks and pick up everyone's garbage and recyclables!

Ready for recycling!

Reflective Jacket!

Garbage Truck!

Did You Know?
Many sanitation workers are super strong! Lots of cities require them to take physical tests to see if they can lift heavy trash cans all day.

Boots!

Firefighters

They put out fires!

When a building is on fire, the fire department shows up to put out the flames and rescue anyone trapped inside! It can be a dangerous job, but firefighters are really brave.

Ready for a ruff, ruff rescue!

28

Helmet!

Fire Resistant Clothing!

Oxygen Mask!

Did You Know?
Most firefighters are also trained in emergency medical services!

29

Everyone's hometown is full of everyday heroes!

Media Lab Books
For inquiries, call 646-838-6637

Copyright 2017 Topix Media Lab

Published by Topix Media Lab
14 Wall Street, Suite 4B
New York, NY 10005

Printed in China

ISBN 10: 1-942556-85-3
ISBN 13: 978-1942556-85-5

CEO Tony Romando

Vice President of Brand Marketing Joy Bomba
Director of Finance Vandana Patel
Director of Sales and New Markets Tom Mifsud
Manufacturing Director Nancy Puskuldjian
Financial Analyst Matthew Quinn
Brand Marketing Assistant Taylor Hamilton

Editor-in-Chief Jeff Ashworth
Creative Director Steven Charny
Photo Director Dave Weiss
Managing Editor Courtney Kerrigan
Senior Editors Tim Baker, James Ellis

Content Editor Kaytie Norman
Content Designer Rebecca Stone
Content Photo Editor Catherine Armanasco
Art Director Susan Dazzo
Assistant Managing Editor Holland Baker
Senior Designer Michelle Lock
Designer Danielle Santucci
Assistant Photo Editor Jessica Ariel Wendroff
Assistant Editors Trevor Courneen, Alicia Kort
Editorial Assistants Mira Braneck, Brendan Luke,
Rachel Philips, Jordan Reisman

Co-Founders Bob Lee, Tony Romando

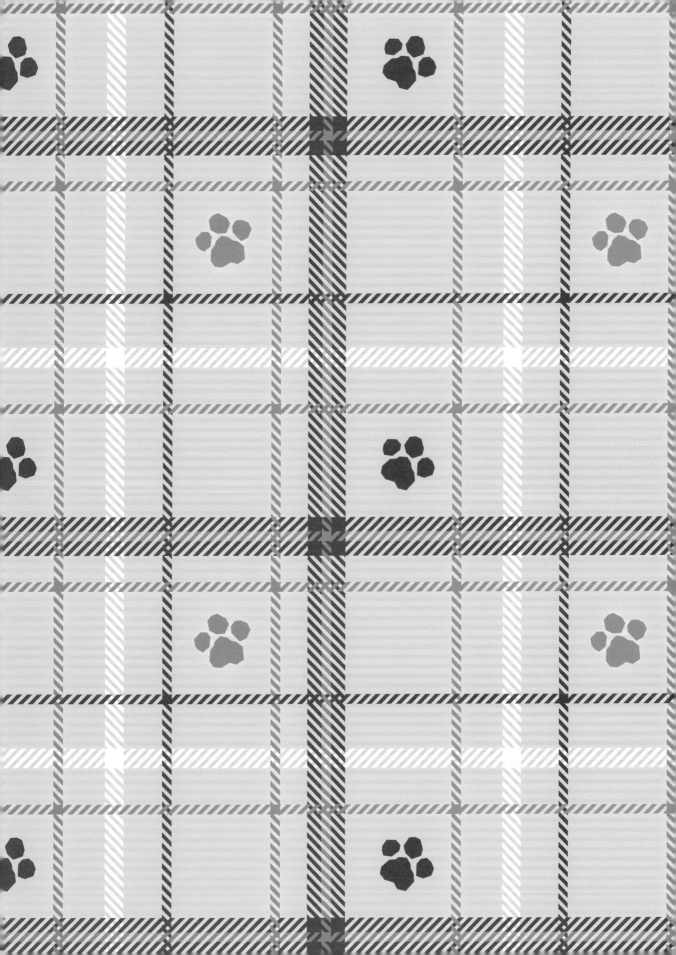

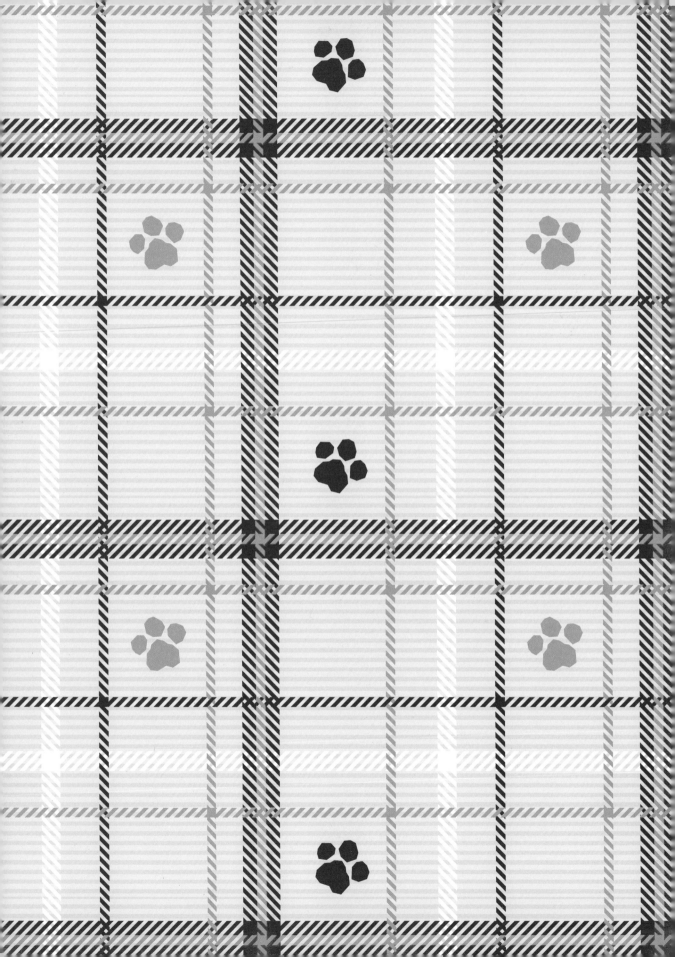